Thank You, Jesus!

The Story of Jesus and One Thankful Man

We are grateful to the following team of authors for their contributions to *God Loves Me*, a Bible story program for young children. This Bible story, one of a series of fifty-two, was written by Patricia L. Nederveld, managing editor for CRC Publications. Suggestions for using this book were developed by Jesslyn DeBoer, a freelance author from Grand Rapids, Michigan. Yvonne Van Ee, an early childhood educator, served as project consultant and wrote *God Loves Me*, the program guide that accompanies this series of Bible storybooks.

Nederveld has served as a consultant to Title I early childhood programs in Colorado. She has extensive experience as a writer, teacher, and consultant for federally funded preschool, kindergarten, and early childhood programs in Colorado, Texas, Michigan, Florida, Missouri, and Washington, using the *High/Scope* Education Research Foundation curriculum. In addition to writing the *Bible Footprints* church curriculum for four- and five-year-olds, Nederveld edited the revised *Threes* curriculum and the first edition of preschool through second grade materials for the *LiFE* curriculum, all published by CRC Publications.

DeBoer has served as a church preschool leader and as coauthor of the preschool-kindergarten materials for the *LiFE* curriculum published by CRC Publications. She has also written K-6 science and health curriculum for Christian Schools International, Grand Rapids, Michigan, and inspirational gift books for Zondervan Publishing House.

Van Ee is a professor and early childhood program advisor in the Education Department at Calvin College, Grand Rapids, Michigan. She has served as curriculum author and consultant for Christian Schools International and wrote the original *Story Hour* organization manual and curriculum materials for fours and fives.

Photo on page 5: Jo Brown/Nick Smel/Tony Stone Images; photo on page 20: Comstock.

Library of Congress Cataloging-in-Publication Data

Nederveld, Patricia L., 1944-
      Thank You, Jesus!: the story of Jesus and one thankful man/Patricia L. Nederveld.
         p. cm. — (God loves me; bk. 36)
     Summary: A simple retelling of the story in which Jesus heals ten
lepers, but only one returns to thank him. Includes follow-up activities.
      ISBN 1-56212-305-X
      1. Healing of the ten lepers (Miracle)—Juvenile literature.
[1. Healing of the ten lepers (Miracle). 2. Jesus Christ—Miracles.
3. Bible stories—N.T.] I. Title. II. Series: Nederveld, Patricia L., 1944-
God loves me; bk. 36.
BT367.H47N43 1998
232.9'55—dc21
                                         97-52790
                                         CIP
                                         AC

10 9 8 7 6 5 4 3 2 1

Thank You, Jesus!
The Story of Jesus and One Thankful Man

PATRICIA L. NEDERVELD

ILLUSTRATIONS BY ANGELA JARECKI

CRC Publications
Grand Rapids, Michigan

This is a story from God's book, the Bible.

It's for say name(s) of
your child(ren).

It's for me too!

Luke 17:11-19

People!
People!
People!
Everywhere Jesus
went there were
people! People
who wanted to
listen to Jesus.
Sick people who
knew Jesus could
make them well.

7

One. Two. Three. Four. Five. Six. Seven. Eight. Nine. Ten! Ten very sick men came as close to Jesus as they dared. You see, they didn't want Jesus to get sick too.

But they knew Jesus could make them well again. So they shouted as loud as they could, "Jesus! Jesus! Help us!"

Jesus stopped to talk to the ten sick men. He felt sorry for them. "Go to the priests and show them that you are not sick anymore," said Jesus.

One. Two. Three. Four. Five. Six. Seven. Eight. Nine. Ten! The men obeyed Jesus. And as they ran to find the priests, they looked at themselves. They were healthy again!

One. Two. Three. Four. Five. Six. Seven. Eight. Nine! Nine happy men kept running. But one happy man turned around. He ran back to Jesus.

I wonder if you know why . . .

"Thank you!
Thank you,
Jesus!"
he said.

wonder if you have something to thank Jesus for . . .

Dear Jesus, thank you for loving us and taking care of us! Amen.

Suggestions for Follow-up

Opening

As you greet your little ones by name today, thank them for coming. Throughout your time together, look for opportunities to thank the children for helping, and encourage them to say thank you too.

Your little ones enjoy many good gifts from God. Collect pictures from magazines, catalogs, and store flyers of things for which they can give thanks: mommies and daddies, friends, brothers and sisters, pets, food, clothing, toys, homes, churches, and so forth. Mount the pictures on large index cards or on half sheets of construction paper. Laminate if you wish to make them more durable and easy to clean. Spread the pictures on the floor as you invite children to form a circle. Explain that you are going to thank God for all the good things he gives each one. Invite each child to choose one picture and to say a simple prayer: "Thank you, Jesus. Amen."

Learning Through Play

Learning through play is the best way! The following activity suggestions are meant to help you provide props and experiences that will invite the children to play their way into the Scripture story and its simple truth. Try to provide plenty of time for the children to choose their own activities and to play individually. Use group activities sparingly—little ones learn most comfortably with a minimum of structure.

1. Let children enjoy cooking with real food in the housekeeping center. Set out small bowls of dry cereal in various shapes and colors, raisins, chocolate chips or M&Ms, soup crackers, and so forth. Encourage them to prepare a treat for themselves and to serve you and their friends. Talk about how good it feels to be a thankful person and how happy Jesus is when we remember to thank him. Say or sing this simple prayer (music in Songs Section, *God Loves Me* program guide):

   God is great, and God is good.
   Let us thank him for this food. Amen.
   —Anonymous

2. Prepare your art area for painting—cover the table with a plastic shower curtain or newspaper, set out a dishpan of warm soapy water, and provide paper towels and paint smocks. Ahead of time, copy the praying hands poster (see Pattern O, Patterns Section, *God Loves Me* program guide) on bright colored card stock. Pour contrasting colored tempera paint in shallow aluminum pie plates. Show your little ones how to dip their hands in the paint and stamp their hand prints over the outline of the hands on the poster. Don't worry if the prints don't line up perfectly with the sketch. Dip hands into the soapy water, and dry with paper towels. Read the verse from Psalm 106 to your little ones, and invite them to fold their hands as you thank God for his goodness.

3. Bring a small baby blanket and a soft Nerf ball. Have older children stand spaced around the blanket holding the edges. Invite one child to toss the ball into the center of the blanket while you say, "Thank you, Jesus, for loving [child's name]." Show the children how to wiggle the blanket to bounce the ball. After several bounces or when the ball falls off, choose another child to toss the ball and be the subject of thanksgiving. Have younger children sit in a circle and roll the ball to each other as you give thanks for one child at a time.

> —Adapted from *100 More Activities for Preschoolers*, © 1991, David C. Cook Publishing Co. Reproduced by written permission. May not be further reproduced.

4. Invite your little ones to thank and praise God with music and movement. Provide strips of crepe paper or brightly colored fabric to twirl to the rhythm of "For Health and Strength" (Songs Section, *God Loves Me* program guide). Add bells to the streamers if you wish. Play the song on the piano or guitar, and sing these words together:

> *For health and strength and daily food we praise your name, O Lord!*
> —Traditional

Older children may enjoy adding their own words. For example, they could sing: "For moms and dads and friendly pets . . . " or "For coats and shoes and cozy beds . . . "

Closing

Gather your children close to you, and encircle the group with your arms. Remind your little ones that God loves them very much. Softly sing these stanzas of "God Is So Good" (Songs Section, *God Loves Me* program guide) as your prayer:

> *God is so good . . .*
> *Thank you, dear God . . .*
> —Stanza 1, traditional

At Home

You can encourage your little one to give thanks for the good gifts God gives each day. Clip pictures from magazines, catalogs, and store flyers, and provide snapshots of family members. Assemble the pictures in a small photo album your child can carry in a book bag or keep beside the bed. Or help your little one make a poster collage for your refrigerator by gluing the pictures on a large sheet of construction paper or posterboard. Use quiet time or bedtime or a Sunday afternoon to pray together, giving thanks for each person or thing pictured. Add new pictures as you and your child experience more of God's goodness.

Old Testament Stories

Blue and Green and Purple Too! *The Story of God's Colorful World*

It's a Noisy Place! *The Story of the First Creatures*

Adam and Eve *The Story of the First Man and Woman*

Take Good Care of My World! *The Story of Adam and Eve in the Garden*

A Very Sad Day *The Story of Adam and Eve's Disobedience*

A Rainy, Rainy Day *The Story of Noah*

Count the Stars! *The Story of God's Promise to Abraham and Sarah*

A Girl Named Rebekah *The Story of God's Answer to Abraham*

Two Coats for Joseph *The Story of Young Joseph*

Plenty to Eat *The Story of Joseph and His Brothers*

Safe in a Basket *The Story of Baby Moses*

I'll Do It! *The Story of Moses and the Burning Bush*

Safe at Last! *The Story of Moses and the Red Sea*

What Is It? *The Story of Manna in the Desert*

A Tall Wall *The Story of Jericho*

A Baby for Hannah *The Story of an Answered Prayer*

Samuel! Samuel! *The Story of God's Call to Samuel*

Lions and Bears! *The Story of David the Shepherd Boy*

David and the Giant *The Story of David and Goliath*

A Little Jar of Oil *The Story of Elisha and the Widow*

One, Two, Three, Four, Five, Six, Seven! *The Story of Elisha and Naaman*

A Big Fish Story *The Story of Jonah*

Lions, Lions! *The Story of Daniel*

New Testament Stories

Jesus Is Born! *The Story of Christmas*

Good News! *The Story of the Shepherds*

An Amazing Star! *The Story of the Wise Men*

Waiting, Waiting, Waiting! *The Story of Simeon and Anna*

Who Is This Child? *The Story of Jesus in the Temple*

Follow Me! *The Story of Jesus and His Twelve Helpers*

The Greatest Gift *The Story of Jesus and the Woman at the Well*

A Father's Wish *The Story of Jesus and a Little Boy*

Just Believe! *The Story of Jesus and a Little Girl*

Get Up and Walk! *The Story of Jesus and a Man Who Couldn't Walk*

A Little Lunch *The Story of Jesus and a Hungry Crowd*

A Scary Storm *The Story of Jesus and a Stormy Sea*

Thank You, Jesus! *The Story of Jesus and One Thankful Man*

A Wonderful Sight! *The Story of Jesus and a Man Who Couldn't See*

A Better Thing to Do *The Story of Jesus and Mary and Martha*

A Lost Lamb *The Story of the Good Shepherd*

Come to Me! *The Story of Jesus and the Children*

Have a Great Day! *The Story of Jesus and Zacchaeus*

I Love You, Jesus! *The Story of Mary's Gift to Jesus*

Hosanna! *The Story of Palm Sunday*

The Best Day Ever! *The Story of Easter*

Goodbye—for Now *The Story of Jesus' Return to Heaven*

A Prayer for Peter *The Story of Peter in Prison*

Sad Day, Happy Day! *The Story of Peter and Dorcas*

A New Friend *The Story of Paul's Conversion*

Over the Wall *The Story of Paul's Escape in a Basket*

A Song in the Night *The Story of Paul and Silas in Prison*

A Ride in the Night *The Story of Paul's Escape on Horseback*

The Shipwreck *The Story of Paul's Rescue at Sea*

Holiday Stories

Selected stories from the New Testament to help you celebrate the Christian year

Jesus Is Born! *The Story of Christmas*

Good News! *The Story of the Shepherds*

An Amazing Star! *The Story of the Wise Men*

Hosanna! *The Story of Palm Sunday*

The Best Day Ever! *The Story of Easter*

Goodbye—for Now *The Story of Jesus' Return to Heaven*

These fifty-two books are the heart of *God Loves Me,* a Bible story program designed for young children. Individual books (or the entire set) and the accompanying program guide *God Loves Me* are available from CRC Publications (1-800-333-8300).